a time to get rich!

Adrian Van Eck

> HAVING MONEY, JUST QUIETLY HAVING IT AND KNOWING YOU HAVE IT,
> GIVES YOU SECURITY, A FEW COMFORTS OF LIFE AND PEACE OF MIND.

A TIME TO GET RICH

by Adrian Van Eck

© 1986

The Boggastow Book Company

FORWARD

The theme *and illustrations* of this book have been drawn from The King James Bible - Book of Ecclesiastes, as follows:

"To every thing there is a season, and a time to every purpose under the heaven. . . .**A TIME TO GET**, and a time to lose; a time to keep, and a time to cast away."

"The thing that has been, it is *that* which shall be; and that which is done *is* that which shall be done; and *there is* no new *thing* under the sun."

"Is there *any* thing where of it may be said, See, this *is* new? It hath been already of old time, which was before us."

"There is no remembrance of former *things*; neither shall there be *any* remembrance of *things* that are to come with *those* that shall come after."

"That which hath been is now; and that which is to be hath already been; and God requireth that which is past."

"I said in mine heart concerning the estate of the sons of men, that God might manifest them, and that *they might see that they themselves are beasts.*"

A TIME TO GET RICH
Table of Contents

CHAPTER ONE - 1987-88-1989 (Where We Are Going)

Everything is falling into place now in the Stock Market. For seven long years, we have been telling subscribers to our Newsletter that the 1980's are simply a replay of the 1920's. Each year, more and more People have come around to our way of thinking. . .so that today more than six thousand readers in the U.S., Canada and foreign nations are mentally ready for developments in both the Stock Market and the economy.

But, of course, the really exciting days of the 1980's still lie ahead of us. What we have seen so far is nothing but *preparation for the real thing!* Already lots of People who have listened to the Gloom and Doom warnings are growing tired of waiting for the sky to fall in. Each day more of these People are facing up to

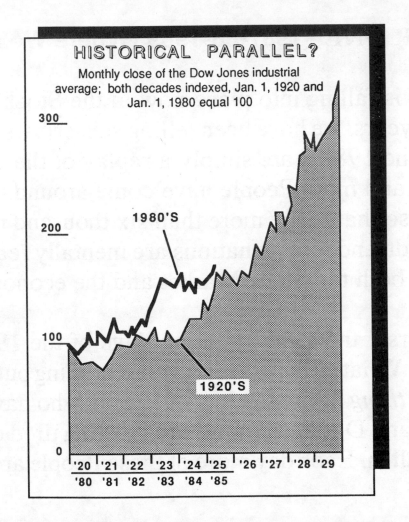

HISTORICAL PARALLEL?

Monthly close of the Dow Jones industrial average; both decades indexed, Jan. 1, 1920 and Jan. 1, 1980 equal 100

1980'S

1920'S

300

200

100

0

'20 '21 '22 '23 '24 '25 '26 '27 '28 '29

'80 '81 '82 '83 '84 '85

the strange new reality: Life in The United States is getting better. Money is being made. The constant talk these past few years that America was on the thin edge of "Another 1929" was just that: *Talk!* 1929? No way! 1926, maybe. *Now comes the GOOD YEARS!*

We got so darned angry in mid-1985 as the business Press filled up with bad talk about "Another 1929 Due Soon." One writer even named the week it was likely to hit...right after Labor Day. *We disagreed. We ran the chart at left* for our subscribers. It showed how very similar 1980-85 had been to 1920-25...and how far up the Market had to travel to reach scary 1929 levels. *This chart helps you understand recent Stock moves sharply UP!*

As our long-term subscribers know, we have little or no patience with the folks on Wall Street who have pumped data about the last week. . .the last month. . .the last year. . .even the last Decade into their computers - and then asked the computers to tell them what is coming next in America and the Western World.

These People suffer from a simple common problem: namely *GROUPTHINK*. They think of history as running back only a year or two or even three. Anything back beyond 1980 is seen as *Ancient History*. They cannot believe anything that happened prior to 1976 could have anything to say to us today about the *future*. So, in many cases, they scrub this "PRE-HISTORY" from their computer memory banks. What a shame. Because in order to understand what has been going on these past seven years. . .what is going on now. . .and what is likely to happen during the rest of 1987, 1988 and 1989, you have to go back and dig very deeply into what actually did go on in the Decade we know as *THE ROARING TWENTIES!*

Lacking this conceptual framework for the 1980's, Wall Streeters in general have been caught by surprise time and time again in recent years. Most of them are suprised anew each waking day. They have no idea *what* is coming tomorrow, no matter what they tell you. If you want to prepare your self and your money for the CHANCE TO GET RICH in the next three years - and the opportunity to hold onto this new wealth after it is all over and many of your own friends have seen their new gains slip out of their hands - then *you really have to take full responsibility yourself for what happens to you.* Maybe you will be lucky and your broker and banker will be aware of the message in this Book. In that case, do not hesitate to talk about what you are going to do with this Person in advance. It helps to get your own goals clearly defined and to decide in advance when "enough is enough" for you. . .so you can get out early. But if you aren't lucky enough to have such a financial advisor, it will be up to you and you alone to grasp what you read on the following pages. . .and use it to set goals for yourself. These goals should include both *Dollar amounts you hope to achieve and Dates that you promise to use as checkpoints along the way.* Always keep these Dollars and Dates in mind !

THERE ARE TWO BASIC FACTS YOU SHOULD KEEP IN MIND ABOUT THE SUPER-BOOM OF THE LATE 1980's ! One is that during the early part of this Superboom - and

by this we mean   1987 - you can make a mistake in timing, even quite a serious error - and *still have things work out to your advantage !* By that we mean that you can decide to buy a stock or a mutual fund right at the very top of a short-term move, only to see it fall away in one of those inevitable sinking spells that brokers like to call "Corrections." (So who do you know that ever likes to be "corrected," for goodness sake ?) But if you hold on tight and close your eyes and keep real quiet, why almost before you know it the "correction" will be over and your stock or mutual fund will be moving up again. . .first to the price you paid and then Golly-Gee to a price high enough so that you can, if you so desire, sell it out for a handsome profit. *You do this once. . .twice. . .three times and you'll be feeling so good about yourself you'll want to tell all your friends and relatives about your good fortune.* You may also tell them to "Come on in. The

Water's Fine !''

Please think carefully before you give in to either of these temptations. It may come as a shock to you when it happens, but most of your friends will NOT be happy with your new-found wealth and success. To begin with, they are apt to chalk it up to luck on your part, and not give you credit - as they should - for initiative and courage. Most likely they will resent every penny you make. And that holds double if you cash some of your gains and use the money in a conspicuous way to buy things like an automobile with your profits.

And if their negative reaction to your profits catches you by surprise, *just wait 'till you see what happens later on,* if you make the mistake of urging them to jump into the Market and join

You can make a mistake early in a climbing
market and recover. But - later on - make
a mistake and the Bear will get you!

you. First off, you'll find that they are not likely to do so for a year or two. . .maybe even *three*! That's just human nature. They are going to see and hear talk in the media every day that the Market is too high and due for a big crash. This will *scare* them. They will sit tight on the sidelines, watching you and growing in their dislike for you more each week. But late in the game, possibly right about the time you are getting out of the Market yourself and cashing in some or all of your profits, they may find the news media full of talk about a "New Age" or a "New Era" of perpetual prosperity. (There's that old HUMAN NATURE at work again!) Should they get into the Market at that time, they may very well *lose* some of their money. And guess whom they are apt to blame: not themselves, certainly. No, it is almost certain that they will blame you. They will remember how you told them repeatedly to get into the market.

Your protests that such talk was in the past. . .two or even three years in the past, "way back in 1987". . .will fall on deaf ears. If the history of earlier Super-Booms is any guide, and we mean the Biggies like the Tulip-Bulb Boom, the South-Sea Bubble and the Florida Land Boom of the early 1920's, then they will begin to drop hints that since *you* were responsible for getting them into Stocks at the very *top,* the least you can do is share some of your own "undeserved lucky wealth" with them, and *make good their losses!*

Probably you will refuse to make good their losses. (We certainly would if we were in your shoes.) It can then be expected that you will have an enemy *for life.* . .someone sure to stab you in the back in a verbal way every chance they get. The best way we know of to avoid *needless* loss of such friends is to avoid bragging about your own profits and resist the temptation to help them by getting them into Stocks.

If they show an interest in your investing, tell them how you read a fascinating book. . .*this one*. And tell them where you bought your copy. Period ! Don't even loan them your copy. Even that could be used against you later on if they fail to act early enough and fail to get out on time ! (If they read their own copy and become a fellow-believer, *that's another matter*. Comparing notes can be fun and helpful to you both. But whether they enter the Market on their own or not, keep *quiet* about your profits. Very rich families here in New England are so discreet about their wealth (whether old or new) that only their tax accountant, their banker, their lawyer and the IRS know for certain that they are rich. *Having money, just quietly having it and knowing you*

HAVING MONEY, JUST QUIETLY HAVING IT AND KNOWING YOU HAVE IT, GIVES YOU SECURITY, A FEW COMFORTS OF LIFE AND PEACE OF MIND.

have it, gives you security, a few comforts of life and peace of mind. On a scale of 1 to 100, these three rank up there at 96 or 97. . .maybe 98. . .even 99 !

*This brings us to our second warning to you: as it gets later in the game. . .1988 and 1989. . .*the problem of timing looms ever more important. We do not pretend that we can do more than draw you a very sketchy picture of those "out" years. The expectation is that we will by then be in a "topping out" period. But as to how high Stocks will go or how long the Market will keep going on up to new highs. . .we don't have those answers yet. (Maybe in a year or two, 1988 and 1989 will emerge clearly and sharply from the fog now swirling all around them.)

But we can warn you, based on a deep knowledge of similar

Super-Booms in the past, that *as we move into the later years, the risk grows. . .first by a factor of 10 and then by a factor of 100 !* What we believe is true now will not be true them. Make a mistake *late* in the Super-Boom and you may get *burned !* One never knows in advance which top may be the final top. Buy on a dip three years from now and you may not get a bargain. . .you may get a permanent loss.   *1987 will be the year of the greatest gains. . .and the least risk !*

CHAPTER TWO
Van Eck's Record (How We Got Here)

MONEY makes the World go 'round. Or at least that part of the World including Western Europe, the Americas, Japan, South Korea and Taiwan. *PEOPLE control money.* Thus it is our belief that if you keep pretty good tabs on MONEY and PEOPLE you will have a good grasp of where the economy is and where it is headed. For the past 10 years, we have made that belief the *basis* of our Newsletter. So far it has not let us down. Nor has it disappointed our subscribers.

Just recently, for example, we received a note from a subscriber who happens to be a Stock Broker in New York State. In it he wrote: "I've been amazed over your ability to foresee trends developing a good bit in advance of the actual event. Your advice has helped me steer many of my clients to the right course in the past three years." *(Note: we are intensely proud of the number of Stock Brokers who read our Forecast Letter today. Some of them have to get the Letter at home, because it contradicts "official" advice from their own firm's research department!)*

The only problem that has turned up so far in using our **PEOPLE PLUS MONEY** Forecast Formula is that it tends to get us out ahead of events just a little bit. We are constantly responding to events that have so far happened only in our own mind *(where we see them so clearly, we sometimes convince ourselves they have already taken place.)* In the beginning, our Forecasts were met with disbelief. . .even sarcasm.

For example, when we issued a "BUY GOLD NOW" message early in 1976, it seemed to many of our readers (who numbered only in the low hundreds at the time) as if we had lost our mind. (And some of them wrote to tell us so.) After all, inflation was down around 2% a year and seemingly headed down. But we told our readers that new developments in MONEY behind the scenes, developments involving powerful PEOPLE in Government and Finance, made it likely that inflation would soar to 20% a year in just a few years.

GOLD WAS $140 AN OUNCE WHEN WE SAID BUY. It slipped and slid to $100 over the next several months, while we kept repeating our new inflation warning. Then, late in 1976, just about on Election Day, the tide began to *turn* for Gold and Inflation. Over the next three years, prices rose at an ever-faster

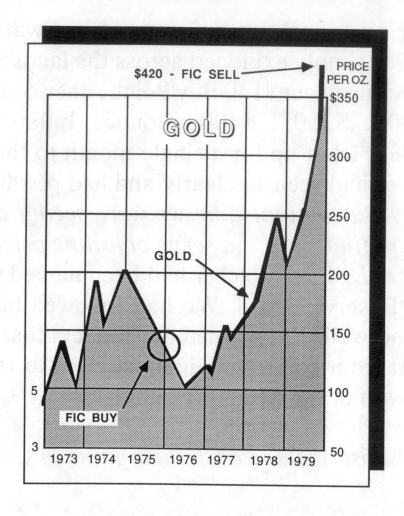

23

rate in America. . .as the very forces we had warned about in January, 1976, simply exploded across the landscape. GOLD rose too. . .back up to our $140 Buy Point. . .then on up to $200. . . $250. . .$300. . .$350. . .$400 an ounce. Inflation hit double digits. . .15%. . .shot up for a single month to the exact 20% annual rate we had seen so clearly and had predicted four full years earlier. *But by that time we were seeing a brand new picture in our mind's eye. . .a scene of falling prices and panic selling in GOLD.* Paul Volcker had been named Chairman of the Federal Reserve Board. We had followed his career and knew his mind well. We warned our readers that he was now likely to shift from controlling interest rates to restricting the runaway growth of the MONEY supply.

We advised subscribers to cash their gains in GOLD. (It had

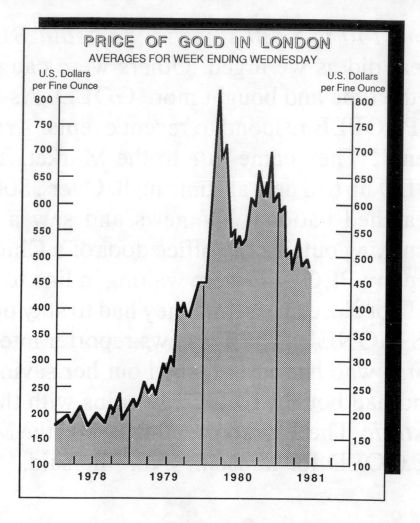

PRICE OF GOLD IN LONDON
AVERAGES FOR WEEK ENDING WEDNESDAY

tripled from $140 to $420 since we had said BUY GOLD.) Some readers did as we urged. Others were caught up in the emotion of the time and bought more GOLD. As usually happens, most PEOPLE respond to recent events. . .rather than to coming events ! They came *late* to the Market. Their buying pushed GOLD up to a new all-time high. Over $800 an oz. One night we watched national TV news and saw a long line of PEOPLE snaking outside the office door of a Chicago GOLD dealer. So many PEOPLE were waiting in line to buy that the dealer could not close at 5 P.M. They had to stay open and take PEOPLE'S MONEY. The TV news reporter interviewed one Chicago nurse who had just cleaned out her savings account - $8,000 - and had bought 10 GOLD coins with the MONEY. *She was ecstatic.* The TV reporter then asked the Manager if he was buying GOLD for himself. "No," he said. "I'm so busy taking care of these folks that I have no time to buy GOLD for my own account." We shook our head. *We knew this had to be the peak of madness. It would be all over within hours, we felt. And, of course it was!* GOLD stalled out just a few days later and began a steep panic decline, just as we had foreseen late in 1979.

Some PEOPLE bought more GOLD as prices fell, thinking it to be just another correction. We knew better and *said so!* WE WARNED THAT WALL STREET HAD MISREAD A STATEMENT BY FED CHAIRMAN VOLCKER, IN WHICH HE SAID THAT HE WOULD NOT IMPOSE *GENERAL* CREDIT CONTROLS. He used his words with the precision of a surgeon, we told readers. If he meant to say NO controls at all, he would not have added the word "general."

It could only mean one thing, we said: *SPECIFIC CREDIT CONTROLS*, just like those imposed by IKE in the early 1950's. The back of inflation would be busted, we warned. Both **GOLD** and **STOCKS** were sure to *collapse*. But when Wall Street discovered how bullish the end of inflation could be, stocks would come back sharply. *Within a month, Volcker imposed specific credit controls. Everything we had foreseen and warned about came to pass.* (It seemed fewer people criticized our **MONEY PLUS PEOPLE** Forecasting Formula after that. In fact, more readers joined our Letter on the advice of their friends.) And thus began the 1980's - a decade we were convinced would be *like the 1920's*!

We correctly predicted that Reagan's historic Tax Reduction program would pass - and that it would *not be inflationary,* as so many others believed! The reason it would not be inflationary, we said, was that Fed Chairman Volcker would restrict the growth of money. He would refuse to buy much in the way of Government bonds, thus forcing private savers to fund the debt. Money would grow tight. The result? We said it would be a virtual *end* to huge annual raises at unionized Big Business manufacturing plants. Workers were signing three-year contracts with 1% a year raises plus cost of living increases. They were expecting paychecks to grow by 15% a year or more. We said they would be lucky to see 5%. *When the nation's Air Traffic Controllers struck, we told readers Pres. Reagan would fire them all and never rehire them.* (We'll tell you how we knew that later on.) And we said that plus Volcker's tight money would end the rash of strikes that pushed inflation up. *Everything happened exactly as we had foreseen. (And again more of our subscribers became believers in our MONEY PLUS PEOPLE Forecasting Formula !)*

There were, of course, opposing Forecasts. Indeed we found ourselves a lone voice here in the New England wilderness most of the time. In 1980, for example, we were all alone in America or the rest of the World, for that matter, in predicting that a soaring U.S. Dollar would be the Number One Story of 1981. We even named a target value - 3 Marks per Dollar. At the time of our Forecast, the Dollar was trading at just under 2 Marks and the idea of a 3-Mark Dollar was seen by Wall Street analysts as quite unlikely. As so often happens, *we were right-on with our Forecast* but a little premature. (We constantly warn subscribers of this habit we have of seeing coming events so clearly that we think they are closer in time than they eventually prove to be !)

In 1981, Wall Street's favorite guru, Henry Kaufman, dazzled and delighted the Media and Very Rich Customers at a series of breakfast press briefings. We disagreed with him every time! Inflation would head upward, he said. (We said it would trend down.) He predicted a 25% prime by the end of 1981. (We said rates would be down 50% in 4 years.) We warned that *deflation* might result from overkill by the Fed. And we said that the long *housing-price* boom of the 1970's was doomed. We even gave the month it would end: *August, 1981*. We hit the end of the Housing Boom on the nose. It ended just before Labor Day, 1981. But we were a little early with our Deflation warning. America was 90 days in to 1982 before the first month of *declining prices* shocked Wall Street right out of its shoes.

The 1982 recession and bear market brought the first of many claims that *Another 1929* was close at hand. *We said otherwise.* In the Spring of 1982, we spoke of a Recovery soon that would turn into a Boom quickly. We said interest rates were being held up by mirrors and hot air. . .and told our readers *rates would collapse by Fall.* We also pointed out that Bull Markets had often begun in the middle of the second year of a new Presidency . . .and noted mid-1982 was such a time !

THE KIPLINGER LETTER, a famous Washington-based Letter, seemed to speak for just about everyone in July of 1982 when they said that interest rates had gone about as low as they were going to go and the Stock Market had gone about as high as it was going to go for some time. In fact, Kiplinger suggested that stocks were about to go down in anticipation of *rising interest rates.* We've got to admit: we felt very lonely right at the moment. We had read Kiplinger ourselves for a lot of years. . . since the mid-1950's. No one had more respect for Kiplinger than we did. But, darn it, *our own studies and our own instincts said that this one time they were dead wrong. So we had to call it as we saw it. We told our subscribers that we stood by our belief that America was then repeating the inflation-smashing recession of the early 1920's and that a major decline in interest rates was close at hand.* (We didn't realize it then, but the decline in interest rates we were predicting had already begun a few days earlier.)

As we had said with such confidence would happen, interest rates *collapsed* before the election. In four months, they fell 4 points. NOT RECOGNIZING THE PARALLEL TO THE EARLY 1920's, *WALL STREET HIT THE PANIC*

BUTTON. THEY THOUGHT RATES WERE FALLING BECAUSE WE HAD BEGUN A NEW 1929 - A NEW DEPRESSION. (IT WAS TO BECOME A FAMILIAR THEME ON WALL STREET, BEING REPEATED MANY TIMES DURING THE 4 YEARS TO COME.) In November we said: "The stock market has just completed its worst day since the terrible collapse in October, 1929. . .Let's examine the very important difference between now and 1929. *We are now almost 17 years past the time (Feb. 1966) when the Dow first reached 1,000. Seventeen years! In those 17 years, the cost of living has just about tripled in America.*

So, adjusted for inflation, you could say that 1,000 on the Dow today equals a 1966 level equal to 333. That's a 67% decline. What's more, the Stock Market has made a run at the 1,000

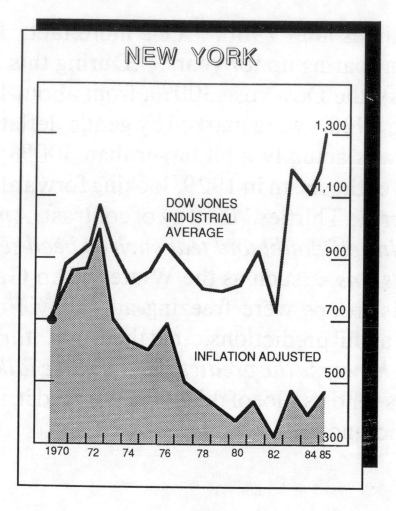

NEW YORK

DOW JONES
INDUSTRIAL
AVERAGE

INFLATION ADJUSTED

1,300
1,100
900
700
500
300

1970 72 74 76 78 80 82 84 85

level several times after 1966. . .One more fact: In 1929, the Dow had been roaring up for years. . .During this Bull Market (of the 1920's), the Dow rose 300%, from about 100 to about 400. Since the 1920's were marked by gentle deflation, the gain in real terms was actually a bit larger than 300%. . .The U.S. was mad with enthusiasm in 1929, looking forward to what was to be 'The Terrific Thirties.' By way of contrast, *America today is wallowing in self-doubt and fear such as been seen only on a very few occasions*. . .such as the Winter when George Washington and his troops were freezing at Valley Forge. People seem to crave awful predictions. . .eat them up. . .thrive on them ! *It seems as if the worse the prediction, the more folks agree with it.* Subscribers send us a lot of this stuff. We read it, smile and file it away." (End quote.)

Like Chicken Little, some People worry a lot that "The Sky Is Falling!." They are missing a chance to Get Rich!

Of course, it wasn't just lower interest rates and a review of the Stock Boom of the 1920's that dominated our predictions in that crucial year of 1982. We also told subscribers (back in March of 1982) that: "THE RECOVERY, WHEN IT COMES, WILL *NOT* BRING A RESUMPTION OF DOUBLE-DIGIT INFLATION - AS SO MANY INVESTORS AND BUSINESSMEN NOW FEAR! *SO FAR, THE ECONOMY HAS BEEN FOLLOWING A COURSE REMARKABLY SIMILAR TO THE EARLY 1920's...*

Somehow all of this history has been forgotten. Probably that's why so many People do not now understand or believe that the current economic conditions have traditionally been the PRELUDE to a real boom...not a phony boom where unit sales stay even while Dollar sales go up....but just the opposite - *a boom where Dollar* sales stay even but unit sales go up each year." (End quote from March, 1982.) Of course, *this wasn't our first bullish prediction of 1982.* Two months earlier we said: **"WE PROMISED YOU A COUPLE OF BLOCKBUSTER PREDICTIONS. HERE THEY ARE: FIRST** -- *this recession is not going to last much longer...The timing of the turn is not so important as the angle of the upturn. The angle will be very steep. The recovery, led by explosive growth in defense spending, will be breath-taking in its power and momentum.* **SECOND:** Don't waste your time worrying about the new business upturn bringing a confrontation in the Money Markets ...*Lower inflation* will allow a boom with moderate M1 growth. Interest rates will continue to decline for months to come. *Wall Street will BOOM despite itself."* (End quote.)

IT ALL DID HAPPEN PRECISELY AS WE PREDICTED IT FOR OUR SUBSCRIBERS (WHOSE NUMBERS KEPT GROWING AS BROKERS, BANKERS, BUSINESSMEN AND INVESTORS TOLD THEIR FRIENDS ABOUT OUR *RECORD*). Later on, advisors would come out of the woodwork and claim that their writings, *properly interpreted*, had seen the upturn coming. You didn't have to interpret *our* work. We made our forecasts so clear that no one needed any special training in finance to follow them! As we said repeatedly, the 1980's closely followed the 1920's. *You saw (Chart) how right our predictions were!*

Then, too, there was our strange ability to read Fed Chairman Paul Volcker's mind. Late in 1983, the business media was packed with predictions that the Fed would loosen money for the

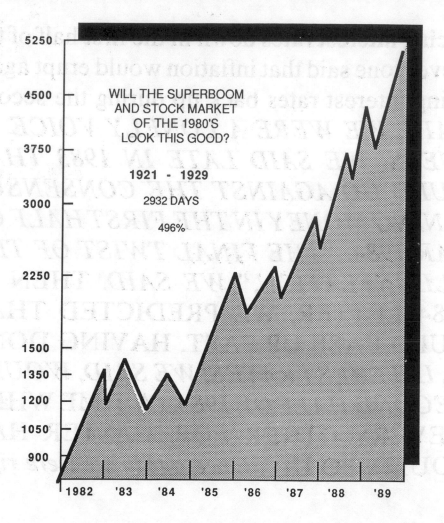

WILL THE SUPERBOOM
AND STOCK MARKET
OF THE 1980'S
LOOK THIS GOOD?

1921 - 1929

2932 DAYS

496%

This Chart shows
the Bull Market
of the 1920's
recast in 1980's
terms. We ran
it in our
Newsletter
several times
starting in
1982. Isn't it
fascinating?

Election Year, forcing interest rates down in the first half of the year. But, almost everyone said that inflation would erupt again in mid-1984, forcing interest rates back up during the second half! *ONCE AGAIN, WE WERE A LONELY VOICE IN THE WILDERNESS. WE SAID LATE IN 1983 THAT VOLCKER WOULD GO AGAINST THE CONSENSUS VIEW - TIGHTENING MONEY IN THE FIRST HALF OF ELECTION-YEAR 1984. "THE FINAL TWIST OF THE SCREW TO KILL INFLATION," WE SAID.* THEN IN OUR JUNE, 1984 LETTER, WE PREDICTED THAT VOLCKER WOULD EASE UP FAST, HAVING DONE IN INFLATION. *INTEREST RATES, WE SAID, WOULD FALL IN THE SECOND HALF OF 1984.* (A TIME WHEN JUST ABOUT EVERY OTHER FORECASTER HAD SAID THEY WOULD GO UP.) *Once again we were right*

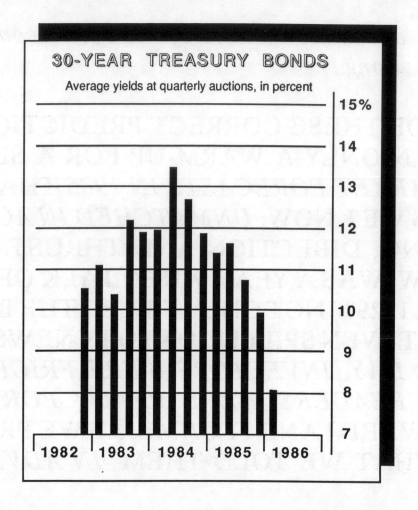

30-YEAR TREASURY BONDS

Average yields at quarterly auctions, in percent

1982   1983   1984   1985   1986

43

both times - and almost 100% of the other economic fore-casters were wrong!

BUT ALL OF THESE CORRECT PREDICTIONS MAY HAVE BEEN ONLY A WARM-UP FOR A SERIES OF *STOCK MARKET FORECASTS IN 1985* THAT WERE, SO FAR AS WE KNOW, *UNMATCHED IN ACCURACY* FOR TIMING, DIRECTION AND THRUST. 1985, AS YOU KNOW, WAS A YEAR WHEN TALK OF "IS THIS ANOTHER 1929?" NOT ONLY FILLED THE BUSINESS MEDIA...IT EVEN SPILLED ONTO TV NEWS SHOWS. *BY LABOR DAY, INVESTORS WERE FRIGHTENED! BUT OUR READERS WERE READY FOR A FAST MOVE UPWARD! AND IT CAME, AS WE PROMISED. HERE'S WHAT WE TOLD THEM -IN ADVANCE OF*

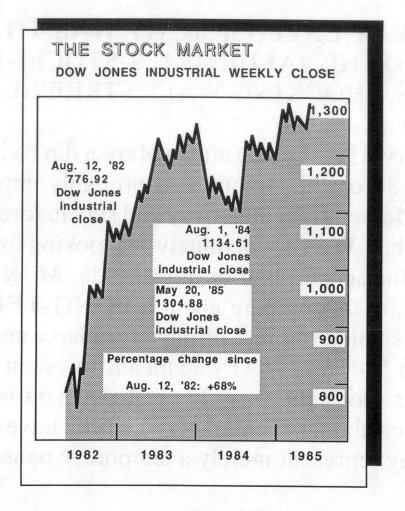

THE STOCK MARKET

DOW JONES INDUSTRIAL WEEKLY CLOSE

Aug. 12, '82
776.92
Dow Jones
industrial
close

Aug. 1, '84
1134.61
Dow Jones
industrial close

May 20, '85
1304.88
Dow Jones
industrial close

Percentage change since
Aug. 12, '82: +68%

1,300

1,200

1,100

1,000

900

800

1982   1983   1984   1985

THE MARKET EXPLOSION. (IT WAS TO ADD $400 BILLION TO THE VALUE OF U.S. STOCKS IN UNDER 5 MONTHS, SHOCKING WALL STREET.):

In our January, 1985 Letter (after a Market dip had taken stocks as low as 1134 on the Dow): "It is probably impossible for a major Bull Market to get underway and stay in force while bond rates are high. . .We very definitely are looking for lower bond yields over the second half of this decade. *Much lower bond yields!* We are talking here about a LONG-TERM MOVE, perhaps consuming the rest of this Decade. . . .and *a target of 3,000 on the Dow by 1989* by no means rules out shorter-term bear markets along the way. It's just that you won't have to worry so much about bear markets when you have a pretty clear idea that they represent merely a temporary pause on the long upward slope." (End quote.) By August the Market was up 150 points and talk of A New 1929 was dominating Wall Street chatter. *We disagreed strongly*. In August we again ran a chart we'd been using since 1982. It showed what the Bull Market of the 1920's would really look like translated into prices of the 1980's. And we said: "RIGHT NOW THE DOW WOULD HAVE TO BE BREAKING INTO NEW HIGH GROUND SOMEWHERE NEAR 1,350. . .IT MAY BE A CO-INCIDENCE. . .BUT THE DOW HAS JUST BROKEN INTO NEW HIGH GROUND NOT THAT FAR FROM 1,350. . .If the similarities should continue *the Dow would take off from this point and blast into orbit by 1986 !*" (End quote.)

We also included in our August Letter a chart by Robert Prechter of the ELLIOTT WAVE THEORIST. His technical studies confirmed our view (using PEOPLE, MONEY AND HISTORY). He showed the Dow breaking out on the upside in late 1985 and 1986, reaching 2,400 before a serious correction begins. This was heady stuff! We concluded (again August, 1985): "All of our *comments have been based on. . .the 'itch' People have to find ways to make profits. . .*We think there is an historical link to 1925." (End quote) SO CONVINCED WERE WE THAT IT WAS A TIME TO *BUY AND NOT TO SELL* THAT IN MID-SEPTEMBER WE LAUNCHED A BRAND-NEW AFFILIATED MINI-LETTER, PROVIDING SPECIFIC INVESTMENT CHOICES. The Dow was still around 1300 then. Within days it was roaring upward. *Within 60 days our choices showed gains of 73% and even 176%.* By mid-December, 1985 - during a period that other forecasters said would mark a repeat of the late-1929

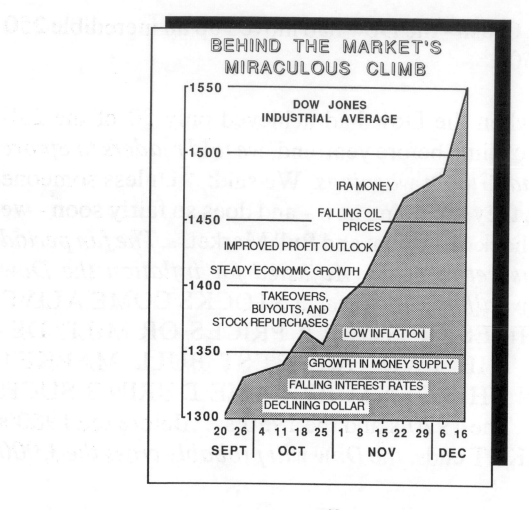

BEHIND THE MARKET'S
MIRACULOUS CLIMB

DOW JONES
INDUSTRIAL AVERAGE

IRA MONEY

FALLING OIL
PRICES

IMPROVED PROFIT OUTLOOK

STEADY ECONOMIC GROWTH

TAKEOVERS,
BUYOUTS, AND
STOCK REPURCHASES

LOW INFLATION

GROWTH IN MONEY SUPPLY

FALLING INTEREST RATES

DECLINING DOLLAR

1550
1500
1450
1400
1350
1300

20 26 | 4 11 18 25 | 1 8 15 22 29 | 6 16
SEPT | OCT | NOV | DEC

49

Stock Market Crash - the Dow had moved up an incredible 250 points to 1,550 !

In October, when the Dow had achieved only 50 of the 250 points it was to climb before year-end, *we told readers to ignore the Doom-And-Gloom warnings.* We said: "Unless someone changes what they are doing now - and does so fairly soon - we are in for one heck of a Boom and Bull Market...*The fun period for stocks has yet to begin. Adjusted for inflation the Dow stands at only half its 1966 level...*STOCKS COME ALIVE DURING TIMES OF STABLE PRICES OR MILD DE-FLATION! THE TWO GREATEST BULL MARKET SURGES IN THIS CENTURY CAME DURING SUCH PERIODS...The 1920's and the 1950's...Before the 1980's BULL MARKET ends, the *Dow will probably cross the 3,000* *line.* It will be 1926-1928 all over again. Let the Superboom Begin ! (End quote from October, 1985.)

We have urged subscribers to our Letters - and we now urge you: KEEP THIS UNBELIEVABLY BULLISH PICTURE OF 1987-1989 FIRMLY IN MIND. . .EVEN IF, AS WE EXPECT, THE STOCK MARKET SUFFERS PERIODIC QUICK, NASTY CORRECTIONS THAT GET THE GLOOM-AND-DOOM FOLKS WHOOPING IT UP AND HOLLERING THAT, AT LAST, 1929 IS HERE AGAIN. *(It is by no means certain that we even have to have what is popularly called "Another 1929" - as we will discuss in a later Chapter.)*

CHAPTER THREE
Why A Big Boom Every 30 Years?

We are not economic technicians. We don't have any rigid framework that we use to make financial forecasts. Rather, we look to such factors as emotional momentum. WHAT PEOPLE DO WITH THEIR MONEY ! That's what interests us. But you cannot look objectively at the economic history of The United States of America without seeing *a major pattern repeating itself.*

America had uncommon economic booms in the 1860's, the 1890's, the 1920's and the 1950's. In each case, many new fortunes were made. There were a lot of chances to GET RICH.

Why every 30 years ? Common sense seems to lead us towards a simple generational theory. Some young men and women marry before they are 20 and start their families. Others marry during their Twenties...and begin families. By the age of 30, and this can be proven quickly by a glance at the available statistics, the majority of young men and women who plan to get married and start a family have done so.

What this means, quite simply, is that after 30 years have gone by *we have in place a whole new generation of hopeful, optimistic young men and women who do not have personal memories of losing money in an economic SUPER-BOOM.* Thus conditions are ripe for a new **SUPER-BOOM** to come along. It can be fed by the expectations of this new generation.

(Remember not so long ago when the rallying cry of America's Young was: "Don't Trust Anyone Over 30 !") Here again you have a fairly concrete example of how the period *THIRTY YEARS* LONG is instinctively seen as a generational dividing line in America.

What this means is that by the time the "Roaring Twenties" rolled around, America was being pushed and driven by a Generation that either had no real memories of "The Gay Nineties" or had decided that the boom-and-bust years of that long-ago decade had no message at all for the 1920's.

Of course, events proved them wrong. *The Big Super-Boom of the 1920's did indeed have something in common with that of*

After each
30-year
Period, the
previous
SuperBoom
seems like
ancient
history.
Then it
happens
all over
again!

the 1890's. And that element was its swift, unpleasant ending!

After the 1920's hit a peak (1929), the bad times that followed were so unpleasant and lasted so long (really until World War II stimulated the economy again in the early 1940's) that *the new Generation taking Power in the 1950's still had vivid personal memories of the "Morning After" years.* And so it happened that when a Super-Boom got underway pretty much on schedule during the 1950's, a rather surprising and unusual response developed. Presidents Harry S. Truman and Dwight D. Eisenhower very sternly resisted letting this Super-Boom get out of hand.

The Public supported strict Government moves to tamp down speculation. Four separate recessions were not only allowed by

Following World War II, President Harry S. Truman used the Army to crush a Railroad strike and break inflation in America.

these Presidents. . .they were encouraged ! Just as in the 1920's, common stocks quadrupled in value. And a lot of People worried that this meant another "Morning After" was at hand. But as events turned out, the stern measures adopted by Presidents Truman and Eisenhower (with the co-operation of equally-prudent Congressional leaders, Bankers, Brokers and Business Executives), left America in such solid financial shape by the end of the 1950's that *still another decade of Super-Boom was piled on top of the 1950's,* with stocks not peaking until 1966 and late 1968 !

The very fact that the economy and stocks set new highs in the 1960's has thrown off America's sense of history when it comes to finance. Very few People actually know or sense the *true underlying 30-year tide* that seems to carry America's economy forward. . .either rising or falling. There is, in fact, a great deal of confusion today as to just where we stand in the larger picture. . . *the long view.*

Probably it is this lost sense of history that accounts for so much of the just-plain-wrong predictions that have bombarded your ears since the 1980's began. Year after year, *the same voices cry out* to warn you and everyone else that "1929 is here again!" Of course, as you know, events have proven them wrong each year. They are at it again *this* year. They will be shouting louder than ever *next* year. And they will be wrong again. But don't get the idea that we are amused by these false prophets. Quite the contrary. We suspect they are doing an enormous amount of damage *in a cumulative manner.* Permit us to explain what we mean:

By the time America moved into the 1980's, it had been not one but *two* 30-year Generations since the last Big Boom-And-Bust Cycle. That means *many* People remember 1929 personally in this day of extended health and long lives. That is normally a very good thing. Such bright-eyed and bushy-tailed Senior Citizens form a reservoir of experience and wisdom that makes them one of this Country's most valuable assets !

But here we have a Senior Generation plus a still-young Middle Generation. . . both of whom remember the last Super-Boom, 30 years ago. And what do they remember ? A very important fact: If America has the political and economic will, it can avoid the bad after-effect of a Super-Boom just by not permitting speculative excesses to develop during the boom itself! Okay. That's good to remember. . .so long as they remember the *whole* message. If, as can happen, all they choose to recall is that the last Super-Boom did *not* end with Bad Times, they can delude themselves into thinking there is no risk at all involved with a Big Boom.

We can think of nothing quite so likely to make People *lose their fear* of a Super-Boom as will these constantly repeated false warnings of "another 1929". Each time such a warning message is carried in the newspapers and on television news programs – and the most recent time was *early in 1986* when a notorious prophet of Gloom and Doom triggered a brief but nasty decline in stocks - *it grows less and less likely that People will respond correctly to a real time of danger, should one materialize late in the 1980's.* (It is simply the oft-told tale of "The Boy Who Cried

Wolf Too Often.")

And so we urge you: burn the correct historical view of America in your memory. Remember that in the 1860's, the 1890's and the 1920's America had *roaring Super-Booms* - each followed by a most-unpleasant "morning after." But the Super-Boom of the 1950's was followed by *an even Bigger Boom !* Much of the reason for the success of the 1950's in *avoiding* the kinds of speculative excesses that lead to later troubles stems from the active fears of that time. . .fears about 1929 ! Should the False Prophets, with their repeated warnings about 1929, cause us to lose our fear of another 1929, *we most likely will revert back to speculative instincts of earlier Ages.* And when that happens, we really would be in danger of a serious "morning after." Later on, in another Chapter, we will explore the odds on a Happy

Ending vs. a Sad Ending. But, for now, let's concentrate not on the ending, but on the beginning and *the coming HEART of this new Super-Boom!*

CHAPTER FOUR
Back To The Normalcy Of Zero Inflation

During the 1970's, inflation exploded across most of The Western World. In The United States, in particular, this inflation was caused by spending on the War in Viet Nam. Presidents Lyndon Johnson and Richard Nixon both realized that the War was not popular. So, they did not levy taxes to pay for the War. *Instead they simply printed Money to pay the Troops and buy the War Materials.* (Actually, they used a complicated and sophisticated financing technique that involved the Federal Reserve Board buying new Federal Government bonds with Money created out of thin air by the Fed. But *the end result was just the same* as if the Government had simply printed lots of new money.)

President Nixon tried to stop the inflation that came as a result of his "Funny Money" creation by slapping on price and wage controls. He found out - as others have before him - that such controls are just as effective as standing on a beach during a time of incoming tide and *shouting at the ocean waters to "STOP RISING!"*

After a while the price controls stopped working altogether. They grew uncomfortably tight and many People complained about the way the Government was making life difficult. *So the Politicians took off the controls. And, of course, prices shot up fast to make up for the time controls had been on.* It did not take long for People in foreign countries to complain that everything they bought from The United States had suddenly become very expensive. In The Middle East, for example, the nations which had a lot of Oil under the big deserts complained loudly that *the food they were buying from Americans now cost so much* that their children were forced to go to bed hungry. One day, when the People with the Oil got angry enough, they all sent leaders to a meeting. And these leaders decided to *get even* with us for our high prices. They did so by raising the price of the Oil they sold to us. And when they found out they could get away with raising the price of Oil once, they did it a second time. And then a third time. And *soon the price of everything that was made from Oil or used Oil began to go up fast* in The United States and Europe. As we were to discover the hard way, that included just about everything !

When America's prices began to go up faster, People com-

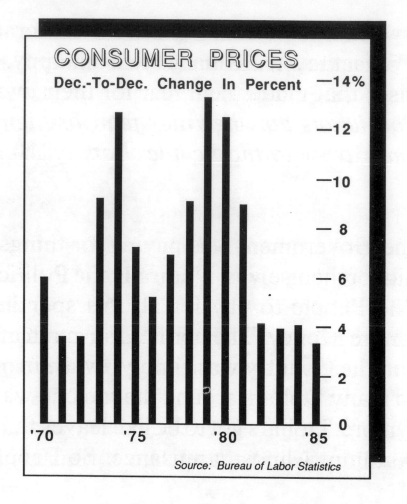

CONSUMER PRICES
Dec.-To-Dec. Change In Percent

Source: Bureau of Labor Statistics

67

plained. And when People complain in a Democracy the Politicians listen. What they heard made them unhappy. They heard grumbling noises that made them fear for their own jobs. *You know what Politicians do when they fear for their own jobs: they give money away to the People. Lots of Money. FREE MONEY!*

Pretty soon the Government was paying for things the People had earlier paid for themselves. Naturally the Politicians did not want to tax the People to pay for all this spending. So they printed some more Money. They printed so much money so fast that pretty soon the Country was simply awash in new Dollars. There were so many Dollars around that no one wanted to hold onto them anymore. Dollars got to be like leaves falling from the trees in the Autumn. Almost a nuisance. So People started to *swap their Dollars for other things. First it was houses.* There were only so many houses standing around. And an awful lot of People were trying to swap Dollars for them. You know what happens when a lot of People are *competing* to swap their Dollars for Houses or anything else. They bid against each other. They keep offering to pay more and more Money for each house. *That makes the price of a House go up.* And when People hear about the price of Houses going up, two things happen pretty quickly: First, the People who have houses to sell start to demand *more Dollars* for their Houses. Secondly, the People who want to buy Houses begin *agreeing* to pay more money for the houses. This turns into a game. And so long as the Government is willing to print more and more money to play the game - sort of like happens in a Monopoly game when the players borrow more and more Money - *the prices keep going up and up!*

After a while, People look around for other things to *swap* their Dollars for. They do so because the word is getting around that with more and more Dollars being created, *the value of each Dollar is going down very fast.* People are afraid that some day their Dollars won't be worth anything at all. And they hope that the things they buy - whatever they are - may *go up* to protect them against this event. So they buy GOLD, because they have been told that will help protect them against this inflation. And they buy Silver. And Diamonds. And Rare Paintings. And they buy farm land. *Lots and lots of farm land.* And the more they buy, the faster prices go up. People soon forget that this is not the way it used to be. They get so used to inflation they begin to think that this must be the way it always was. And even if they don't

During Inflation surges, People squirrel away Money in Gold, Silver, Diamonds and Rare Paintings. This can be costly later when Inflation ends.

believe that, *they began to think this is the way it always will be from now on. Forever and ever!*

It's a shame when People start to think like that. They do strange things. *They borrow a lot of money, thinking it will be easy to pay it back later when inflation has pushed their income up so high that it will be very easy for them to take care of the loan.* And they pay more for things - like houses - than they really think they ought to pay, just because they are so sure that some day, later on, they will find someone to buy it from them at an even more ridiculous price.

The saddest part of all this is that most People really believe this is something *NEW* - something that has never happened before to anyone else. But, of course, that isn't true. Not at all. The

World has seen INFLATION many times, in many places. Each time that it happened, the People then and there were sure it would never end. *But each time, end it DID !*

That's the way it was after the American War of Independence (1775-1781). That's the way it was after America's Civil War (1861-1865). That's the way it was after World Wars I and II. And that's the way it has been since 1980 ! *INFLATION, IT TURNS OUT, IS ABNORMAL AND TEMPORARY.* BUT THE LACK OF INFLATION - EVEN DEFLATION - HAS REALLY BEEN NORMAL AND ALMOST PERM-ANENT DURING THE LAST 200 YEARS. WE ARE NOW BACK IN NORMAL TIMES. MOST PEOPLE DO NOT YET REALIZE THAT. THEY HAVEN'T YET ADJUSTED. THEY KEEP WAITING FOR INFLATION

TO COME BACK. WAITING...AND WAITING...AND WAITING. THEY MAY HAVE A LONG WAIT!

Perhaps the biggest problem with Inflation
is that it encourages People to borrow
Money. When Deflation hits, they can't
pay back the loans...and creditors take
away everything they own. It Is a
lesson learned many times in American
history. It may be learned again!

CHAPTER FIVE
The Innocent Suffer Most !

Farming has long been an important part of what we call The American Way of Life. Thomas Jefferson - author of The Declaration of Independence and third President of The United States - believed deeply that farmers and small farm towns were *vital* to America.

Farmers have maintained the traditional Work Ethic in a time of growing welfare support in our larger cities. Farm towns still have a friendly neighborliness that defies description. You have to actually *live* in a farm community to know first hand just how special these towns can be. No matter how large our cities become, no matter how rich and sophisticated some People become, *it is still the Farmer that is seen as the strength and backbone of our Nation.*

Life on the farm has never been easy. Farmers are born knowing that fact. They accept it. Many Farmers go beyond accepting that fact. They take great pride in the hardships of Farm living. Or, more to the point, they take *uncommon pride in their ability to live with and overcome the natural hardships of Farm living.* Drought. . .insects. . .even floods. All these and more have done their best to defeat Farmers and have failed. But, alas, Man-Made Inflation, Debt and Deflation are succeeding where natural hardships and even disasters have not. . .in hurting Farmers so badly that many of them are *now being forced to give up the Life they hold dear!*

You have seen on the news how farm auctions have ripped Land away from farm families. . .land that in some cases has been in the same family for 120 years or more. (Many of America's family farms date back to the Great Migration West that was *unleashed after the Civil War.*) This is Land and these are families that survived even The Great Depression of The 1930's. That's how terrible today's DEFLATION is on The Farming Heartland of America!

A measure of just how cruel Deflation has been to Farmers comes in the fact that here and there *Farmers have resorted to suicide to try and save the Land for their wives and children.* City folks cannot understand how Land can mean that much to a Farmer. But anyone born and raised on a Farm instinctively understands what drove these desperate men to make the ulti-

mate sacrifice - their own lives - in the hope and belief that Money from their insurance policies (where the law allows it) might pay off or at least reduce the debt on their farms by enough so that the Bankers or Federal Government would *leave their families alone.* TRAGIC !

And the worst part of it is that just about everyone - Farmers, bankers, politicians - *underestimates* just how serious the long-term problem really is. Most People involved in the Farm Deflation situation are under the *false belief* that this situation is probably temporary. . .or that it can be changed by some simple political act. The most popular idea is that a so-called Strong U.S. Dollar has been the villain. *If only the Dollar can be pushed lower, goes this emotional belief, then foreign nations will once again line up America's export docks and Good*

Times will return to Farming communities. Oh, if only it were that easy ! Then America would cure this evil situation. For who among us can stand to see the sight of grown men weeping at farm auctions. . .or even worse - to see widows and orphans weeping on TV news as a farmer who committed suicide to save his Land is laid to rest *before his Time !*

Unfortunately, a cheap Dollar cannot save American Farm-export markets. In country after country, around the World, local farmers have learned how to *increase* their production of food. In some cases it is the development of irrigation systems. In other cases it is the use of the new "miracle seeds" that offer greatly increased yields. But by far the greatest change has been the new awareness by Governments, *even socialist and communist Governments,* that Farmers must be allowed to profit directly from their own hard work on the Land. Communist China, for example, has *busted up its communes* and, in effect, gone back to a system that permits private family farms. The Red Regime now requires only a modest quota of produce to be turned over to the State as a form of rent *(really a tax)* for the Land. The rest of the produce is left in the hands of THE FARMERS. What's more, the Chinese Farmers no longer have to sell their produce to the State at a low, fixed Price. They are allowed to sell it directly to the Public at private, open-air Farm Markets in the towns and cities. *A hustling and bustling commerce has sprung up.* Farmers who adopt improved techniques are fast developing into a prosperous new Middle Class. The total result ? Farm output has doubled in Red China in just 5 years, under this new system. Here is a nation of one billion People that - in the darkest days of communist rule - was faced with chronic starvation on a mass scale. Today it grows all the food it needs, effectively *snuffing out a potentially huge export market for American farm products.* Good news for China. Bad news for U.S. farm towns!

And so it is that the misery of American farmers has spread from their Land to the shops and stores. . .the farm equipment, automobile and truck dealers. . .to local schools and Government. . . and most urgently of all to the local banks in *Farm towns.* Since the larger cities of Farm States depend, too, on whether or not the Farmers prosper, we have a situation that is spreading and growing like a cancer. And *like a cancer it can result in death. . . not just to a Farmer or a Farm but also to Farm towns and Farm States.* To a whole way of Life that stands at the very CENTER of what has from the Beginning been called

AMERICAN ! Fortunately, we see forces at work that can and we think *will* rescue Farm States !

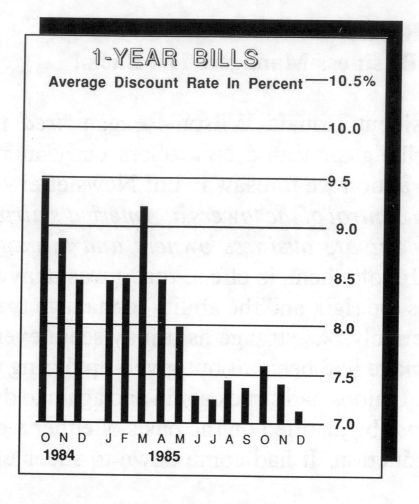

1-YEAR BILLS
Average Discount Rate In Percent ——10.5%

Lower
Interest
Rates may
help
Farmers.
But
another
new force
will help
even more!
(See Ch. 6)

CHAPTER SIX
American Business Managers Hit Back !

When President Ronald Wilson Reagan *fired* thousands of illegally-striking air traffic controllers early in his Administration - an action we foresaw in our Newsletter - *he did more than regain control of the towers at America's airports. He sent a signal to private business owners and managers all over America.* He told them, in effect, that it was okay to seize back from unions the right and the ability to manage their own operations effectively. As strange as it may seem even today, that right to manage had been all-but-given-up during the inflationary 1970's. Unions had struck again and again to demand raises that could *not* be justified on the basis of either worker need or worker production. It had come down to sheer union muscle.

And sometimes it was just exactly that. . .the *physical intimidation* of managers by brutal union "goons" imported from out-of-State just for the duration of a strike. The problem had become most acute in those industries that were either controlled and regulated by the Federal Government or were so big and powerful that the Federal Government stepped in on behalf of union workers whenever management seemed to be on the verge of winning a strike. (That happened in the mid-1970's, when the tire companies were about to *defeat* the Rubber Workers' Union in a long and bitter strike. The White House suddenly intervened and threatened to break Government contracts for tires [a clearly illegal threat] with any company that refused to grant the Union's demands. *Faced with the loss of business from the Armed Forces and the Post Office - huge and essential contracts - the companies gave up and gave in !)* THE

SHARPLY HIGHER WAGE COSTS AND SCANDAL-OUSLY POOR WORK OUTPUT-PER-HOUR RAISED THE COST OF TIRES TO EVERYONE. AND SO IT WENT IN STEEL AND OIL, TRUCKING AND AIR-LINES, COAL AND ALUMINUM! It all came to a head when the air traffic controllers *defied the law* and moved to close down U.S. airports!

This kind of union arrogance had shown up before in U.S. history. Right after World War I, for example, the Boston Police went out on strike in defiance of a Massachusetts law forbidding strikes by public employees. The mayor of Boston was so afraid of **PRO-UNION SENTIMENT** amongst Boston voters that *he did absolutely nothing about the situation, even when looters and rapists started to turn Boston into a criminal's paradise* *and a citizen's hell-on-Earth.* But Governor Calvin Coolidge hesitated not one single minute. Declaring that public employees did not have the right to strike against the Public at any time, under law, this *tough-minded former Vermont farmer* turned Massachusetts politician fired all of the striking Boston policemen. He called up the State Militia to keep order...then hired all new police officers. He vowed that not one of the striking Boston cops would ever wear the blue uniform of an officer of the law again. And *he stunned the union* by making good on that pledge. America knew a real leader when it saw one. Three years later he was in The Oval Office of The White House - President of The United States ! It was a time much like the 1980's were later to be - a time of deflation. As in the 1980's, companies asked unions to take pay cuts, so they could survive. As in the 1980's, the unions responded by going on strike ! Coolidge announced that when the workers got hungry enough *they should go back to work* at the wages their companies could afford to pay. As time passed, that's just what they did. Plants reopened with lower wages and lower prices. They were able to profit and grow. Ronald Reagan was a teen-ager in a town in Illinois as all of this unfolded. *He found a personal hero in Calvin Coolidge.* That was to be important to America 60 years later. And it may now be the economic salvation of farm towns.

It is no accident that *the last tremendous social migration in America - the rush to the suburbs - also came at a time of declining inflation and bitter union resistance to management's requests for reforms.* That was in the 1940's, when Harry S. Truman was in The White House. Unions had been given enormous power by the Federal Government during

Franklin Roosevelt's 13 years in The White House. So *arrogant* had unions become that John L. Lewis' COAL MINERS UNION actually dared strike and shut down the mines during World War II, at a time when American industry ran entirely on *coal power* and needed this energy to produce goods for 11 million men and women fighting overseas !

Truman, upon finding himself President, dropped the first two A-Bombs to end the War. When Russia sent tanks racing into Iran to grab its oil fields, Truman gave the Soviets 48 hours to reverse engines and get out of that nation. Russia backed down and pulled out of Iran, *biding its time to wait for another opportunity* to go for the oil. Then Truman turned to his Number One domestic problem: *postwar strikes by labor unions mad with their own power.*

In those days before the interstate highways were built, Railroads were the only means of moving goods and People. The Rail union struck, shutting down the U.S. The feisty Truman busted the strike. When he did so, he broke the back of inflation in America. An exciting new Age of Growth and Expansion began. Millions of Americans - many of them young veterans just getting married and starting families - rushed out of the cities of America and *bought small homes springing up on what had been farm land.* The Suburbs were born ! A whole new way of living emerged in America.

Now, four decades later, America is on the verge of another important change. Unions that were forced to accept pay cuts and work rule changes a few years ago have elected militant new leaders. These leaders are demanding restored pay levels and a return to *wasteful* work rules.

Some companies are responding by shutting down American manufacturing plants entirely. *But others are moving operations out into farm towns and farm States.* They are hiring Farmers and the sons and daughters of farmers. They are looking for and finding workers who give a day's work for a day's pay. And in doing so they offer a new hope to *save the farm towns.* The success of these farm-town plants - including huge auto assembly plants built by West German and Japanese manufacturers - has attracted attention and interest from America's surging *Service* Industries.

Already one giant New York bank has moved its national credit card operations to the Dakotas, where telephone lines and computers link the workers to the whole nation. . .even the whole World! Others are following. . .insurance and leasing companies, publishers, high-technology firms. In the months to come, a new BOOM may well emerge in Farm States, *allowing farm families to keep their farm roots*. . .even farm part-time if they'd like. The Money flowing in to the farm towns may revive their economies. So too will the business created by migrants from cities and suburbs. . .looking for the Good Old-Fashioned Way Of Life! This may prove to be the biggest development of the late 1980's and early 1990's!

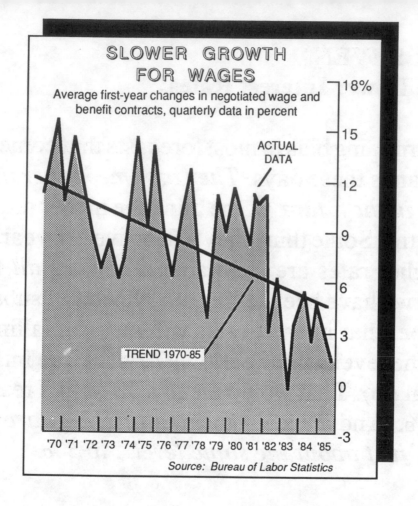

SLOWER GROWTH
FOR WAGES

Average first-year changes in negotiated wage and
benefit contracts, quarterly data in percent

ACTUAL
DATA

TREND 1970-85

'70 '71 '72 '73 '74 '75 '76 '77 '78 '79 '80 '81 '82 '83 '84 '85

Source: Bureau of Labor Statistics

CHAPTER SEVEN
Here Come Lower Interest Rates

There is a surprising bias in most forecasts that come out of Wall street and Banks these days. *They assume higher interest rates for America in the future.* Some think the higher rates will come in a few months. Some think they will arrive in a year. But almost all agree higher rates are inevitable. *They are all wrong!* We believe, and we have been telling our Newletter subscribers this for some time, that interest rates will keep on falling until they get back to the levels of the early 1970's (before inflation really began to heat up). That would mean a 30-year Treasury/rate of around 6½%. And it would mean an *FHA-guaranteed mortgage rate of just about the same level. . .6½%.*

Even this, in our opinion, could possibly prove to be just a temporary way station en route to even lower T-Bond and FHA-mortgage rates. We could see both falling back again to the 5% *level* under certain circumstances !

Such declines in interest rates would extend the Bull Market in Bonds that has been surprising Wall Street for the past 4 years and more. (We told our readers to lock in long-term yields of *14% on 30-year Bonds* at a time when almost everyone else thought we were crazy. We warned subscribers that expectations of still higher rates were doomed to disappointment. *We were proven correct* by events.

The only reason borrowers could justify paying sky-high rates in 1981 (a time when corporate debtors rated Baa by Moody's were paying 17% interest on their long-term bonds) was that they seriously believed *inflation was scheduled to cross right through the 20% a year mark and keep right on going up for years to come. To 25%. To 30%. And even higher. We said at the time such fears were nonsense. Yet even today we hear the same fears expressed. It is still nonsense!* THE FACTORS THAT CAUSED INFLATION IN THE 1970's ARE DEAD. Deflation is now and is likely to continue as the Number One threat to the World economy. Just paying the interest charges on the huge debt outstanding everywhere is *deflationary* all by itself. We cannot understand why it is so hard for Wall Street to understand this simple fact. But in due course, *facts will win out* over myths and false expectations!

It is part and parcel of the myth of coming higher interest rates to believe that the level of interest rates depends on *how much money* the Federal Reserve System chooses to "print" and pour into the nation's Banks. If the link was as close as Wall Street would have you believe, then every move up and down in interest rates in the past decade would have been accurately predicted by economists for Big Banks and Brokerage firms. *The truth is their predictions, for the most part, have been far off the mark.* In fact, we will go so far as to say that YOU COULD HAVE DONE A BETTER JOB PREDICTING INTEREST RATES IN THE 1980's THAN MOST BANKS AND BROKERAGE FIRMS HAVE DONE JUST BY FLIPPING A COIN. Not only were almost all of the economists wrong about the *direction* of rates, they were also wrong about the *speed* in which rates moved.

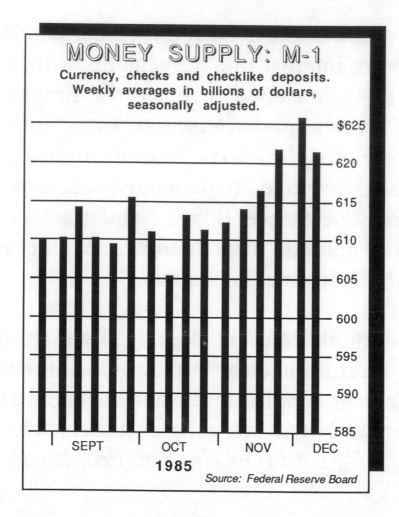

MONEY SUPPLY: M-1

Currency, checks and checklike deposits.
Weekly averages in billions of dollars,
seasonally adjusted.

$625

620

615

610

605

600

595

590

585

SEPT   OCT   NOV   DEC

1985

Source: Federal Reserve Board

Why, then, were we able to correctly forecast both the direction and the speed of interest rate movements with such incredible accuracy? It's because we accepted the simple fact that *psychology had more to do with interest rates than did any decisions by The Federal Reserve System.* Indeed, Paul Volcker himself has acknowledged that on most occasions he and the 7-member Federal Reserve Board (which sets the Fed's own Discount Rate) actually respond to Free Market Rates...rather than trying to determine these rates!

When People think inflation is going sky-high, the Savers demand a bigger return and the borrowers willingly pay it. When inflation is seen as heading lower or even ending altogether, the process reverses. No mystery there. It seems clear to us that *as the reality of DEFLATION sinks in, People will go back to the interest rate levels that have been normal for more than 2000 years. Those rates call for earning 3% a year on your savings and paying 5% a year on your loans.* The 2% difference - known as the spread - is the money that banks and other money-lenders must use to cover their overhead, their losses and (if any is left over) their profit. Before the 1980's end - and maybe a lot sooner than that - the Money Market will *revert back* to traditional levels. This will take a lot of getting used to by everyone involved. . .lenders and borrowers alike. But the Market is too powerful to resist. It will happen! When it does - and even during the time it takes shape - simply incredible changes will take place in the American Economy!

CHAPTER EIGHT
Next Comes A Breath-Taking Boom In Housing !

Many Americans have given up the hope and dream that they will ever own a home of their own. And many American parents have reluctantly *accepted* as a Truth what they constantly read now in magazines or see on TV News shows - namely that this will be the first generation in America's history to fall short of the standard of living they knew as children in their parents' home. *It is disturbing. Even depressing.* The expectation of owning one's own home has been perhaps the strongest single personal ambition shared by Americans from the very day that the Pilgrims set foot on Plymouth Rock during that bitterly cold Winter of 1620-21. *We mean that !* The very first thing Pilgrim survivors did when Spring arrived in 1621 was to choose the locations of their own small cottages. And by the time Autumn arrived and they joined together for America's First Thanksgiving - sharing their harvest with friendly Indians who had taught them such New England tricks as placing a fish in each hole they scooped out to plant corn - the Pilgrims did indeed own and occupy *their own small homes*. When the Mayflower returned to England with the news that there was open land and uncrowded spaces available in Massachusetts, a much larger gathering of Englishmen and their families slowly made plans to follow the original Pilgrims. In 1630, an impressively large convoy of ships brought many more Puritans to Massachusetts. They founded the Town of Boston. And they quickly moved to lay out streets and *erect their own small private homes*.

As the years passed, the trickle of settlers from across the ocean grew into a flood. Some immigrants stayed near the coast-lines. Others headed inland. When they did, their first and sometimes only thought was to get a small *piece of land they could call their own*. . .and to build on that land (sometimes by themselves and often with help from their neighbors) a small dwelling that they could also call their own. *No matter how humble that home, it was the proudest possession a family would own.* And should hardships of any kind threaten a family with the loss of that home, it was seen as a tragedy just as real and as intense as the loss of loved one. It is no wonder that even today - after a decade of rapid construction of apartment buildings and condominiums - some two-thirds of Americans live in their very own single-family home! But, oh, how many more Americans in the "other" one-third yearn to own their own home! And *our message here is that events already in motion make it likely they will before this Decade - the 1980's - draws to a close just a few years from now!*

In 365 years, America has come full cycle. We are back again to the same kind of *restless craving for a better life* that drove the Pilgrims to pick up roots and cross a stormy ocean. We are virtually all immigrants or the descendants of migrants in America. We are descended from People who did not stay and endure misery in the place of their birth. Instead, those with ''get-up-and-go'' simply *got-up-and-went.* There was a saying in early America that when your nearest neighbor was so close that you could hear his axe in the forest, it was time to think about *moving on*, further West. *Open space. Privacy.* Those were sweet words to Americans on the frontier. And whether we like it or not, we carry the blood-line and the genes of those hardy pioneers in us !

The biggest reasons Americans cannot own their own single-family homes in America today have to do with Land and Interest Rates. In the Suburbs developed after World War II, *Land is now scarce and expensive.* In many suburban cities and towns, taxpayers have erected anti-growth barriers to land use and development. Artificial scarcity has driven up the cost of open lots to the point where hardly anyone can afford to build on them. Then, too, the *interest rate* on mortgages has pushed monthly payments so high in relation to incomes that even if the total price of home and land doesn't scare buyers away, the monthly costs of ownership will.

But just when a whole generation of Americans had started to

In early America, People wanted enough Private Space so that they couldn't hear their neighbors!

109

think they would never get a chance to own a home of their own, several lines are converging that says they now can ! To begin with, lots of open land is going begging at low prices in farm communities. . .just waiting for Developers to come in and buy it up. Secondly, the price of lumber has fallen so drastically that the makings of a good home are now within reach. Third: interest rates are about to tumble even lower. Fourth: after years of practice on a smallish scale, American industry has learned how to make real homes at lower costs in factories. Not just mobile homes, but actual *solid houses.* They are being built in sections - just as good quality as on-site homes - and trucked to building sites. Cranes put them together in a single day. It may be the *biggest development in America* since Henry Ford produced his first factory-made auto. Finally, manufacturing and service companies are moving operations out into Farm towns

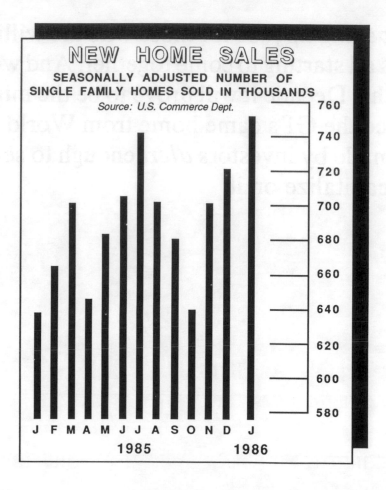

NEW HOME SALES

**SEASONALLY ADJUSTED NUMBER OF
SINGLE FAMILY HOMES SOLD IN THOUSANDS**

Source: U.S. Commerce Dept.

and States - *opening up jobs* for those who are willing to pick up and move. It is all starting to come together. And we believe that by the end of this Decade it will prove to be the mightiest Force unleashed since the GI's came home from World War II. Fortunes will be made by investors *alert* enough to see the trend in advance and capitalize on it.

CHAPTER NINE
The Road For Gold Leads Nowhere!

For more than 10 years Americans have been conditioned to think of a **GOLD BOOM** instantly whenever they hear the phrase **HOUSING BOOM.** That's be cause during the 1970's, *a Housing Boom meant a boom in housing prices.* The Government created more Money. **THAT MONEY FOUND ITS WAY INTO THE BANKS.** And the Banks loaned it out to People who wanted to buy houses. But it did not produce any increase in the *rate of home-building.* Instead it flowed directly into rising home prices. *Pure inflation.* That's what it produced. And inflation led directly to higher prices for Gold. A lot of People came to believe that the link between a good year for housing and *a good year for Gold* could not be broken.

They still think that. Well, you are about to see that link snapped. So beware. Don't let yourself get caught up in hysteria sure to be generated by *promoters of precious metals*. You'll lose money if you do! **THIS TIME THE BOOM IN HOUSING WILL ACTUALLY PRODUCE A SUBSTANTIAL INCREASE IN THE RATE OF HOME-BUILDING!**

Now you will see what happens when the supply of homes increases just as fast as the supply of money available for housing. Or even more likely, you will see what happens when the number of new homes increases *even faster* than the number of Dollars flowing into home loans. Just the reverse of the 1970's will now take place. Too many houses chasing the available Dollars. *That spells* **DEFLATION!** A shocker.

Gold-bugs will refuse to believe it at first. When they see the statistics printed in their favorite financial section or publication, they will rub their eyes and wonder if it is a misprint. Imagine a Housing Boom...with the price of homes actually staying flat or even gently declining! But it won't be a misprint. And it won't be your imagination. It will merely be capitalism at work. Instead of artificial barriers erected by suburban communities trying to *keep out* new home-buyers, you will see competition by farm towns anxious to attract new residents and new businesses.

For these new People will allow Farmers and their communities to survive. It will mean change. America may even change its definition of just what *is* a farmer, as men and women work their fields evenings and weekends, while holding down full-time jobs in offices and plants. But the result will be satisfying.

As for **GOLD**... *it will cease to be a Grand Passion for speculators.* It will seek its own fair level as a long-term store of value...exactly the same role it has enjoyed for hundreds and even thousands of years around the World. *Our own best estimate is that* **GOLD** *will settle somewhere close to $350 an ounce.* We arrive at that level by a crude but effective calculation. Some 50 years ago, Gold was worth *$35 an ounce.* (The U.S. by that time had withdrawn all of its beautiful $20 Gold pieces that contained one ounce of Gold.) There are several tests we have used to arrive at the current value of Gold. Each leads to similar conclusions. For example, you could then take 20 of these coins and exchange them for one of Henry

Ford's new automobiles. Not for one of the many fancy luxury cars on the market then, we hasten to point out. Just for the simple Transportation-on-wheels introduced by America's Master of Low Cost Mass-Production.

Today you can buy some newly-introduced autos for a price around 10 times that of some 1937 Autos. We regard that as a *fair measure of inflation* since then. So we multiply the $35 value of a Gold piece then by ten...and get a current real value of some $350 an ounce. **THAT IS THE LEVEL WE BELIEVE GOLD WILL SETTLE DOWN TO WHEN SPECULATORS FINALLY GET IT STRAIGHT IN THEIR HEADS THAT INFLATION IN AMERICA HAS GIVEN WAY TO MILD DEFLATION!** (Markets often over-shoot targets temporarily at the end of a major decline. So we accept the very real possibility that Gold will at least for a while drop *below $350* an ounce. But that is the level we see as the final target, when all is said and done.) At that price - $350 - **GOLD** will be attractively-priced for what has long been its major attraction. We mean its physical beauty. *Gold jewelry* is likely to become more popular again as it becomes more affordable. And since there are some U.S. Gold mines with rich veins close enough to the surface to permit Gold extraction at under $200 an ounce, *there will still be some profitable investments made in U.S. Gold mines*. But it's the way things will be in Gold during the rest of this Decade at least. So you might as well adjust and prepare for it, in your own best interest!

CHAPTER TEN
A Warning And A Promise About Stocks And Funds !

The biggest gains of all tend to show up in the *middle* stages of a long Bull Market. Unfortunately, these gains scare the living daylights out of most investors. Instead of sharing in them and profiting from them, the average American investor shies away from them. . .*even runs from them.* He or she is usually licking deep emotional wounds from the correction that comes after the First stage of the Bull Market. What so very often happens is that Mr. or Ms. Average Investor has *waited until late in the game* to get into the Market in Stage One. In fact, the historic norm is for them to stay on the sidelines all the way up - no matter how long that takes - because they cannot believe what they are seeing. Then, right at the *very top* (and in more than a few cases just on the other side of the top, as stocks begin their correction and are being touted as *"bargains"* by so many of the investment advisory services), the Investors rush in and BUY.

The usual pattern is to hold the stocks all the way down. Not just to the bottom. . .but for a few weeks after the bottom. They wait until The Second or Middle Stage has begun. . .until their stocks have begun to move up again. *Then they SELL !* At first they are quite proud of themselves. They mistakenly believe that they have shrewdly gotten out of their stocks at or near the peak of a brief and temporary rally in what they have convinced themselves is a new Bear Market. Only later do they realize that they were wrong again in their timing. . .and that stocks, including the stocks they bought near the Top of Stage One and Sold near the Bottom of Stage Two, are *still going up. At first they are just surprised. Possibly even AMUSED. But then the stocks climb back to the level at which they bought them originally... the level that would have let them get out even. And by now they are no longer amused. They are angry!* Angry first at themselves. Then angry at their broker. And finally angry at the Market itself. At first they vow never to get back in the stock market again. But as stocks continue to go up they relent *a little* and decide to move some of their money out of the Money Market Account where they are hoarding it. But this time they are cautious. They move the money into a Bond fund. As time goes on and stocks still keep on climbing - which they are apt to do in the often-long-running Second or Middle Leg of a giant Bull Market - the Investors grow *a little bolder still* and move some of their Money into Equity mutual funds. But they still shy away from investing in individual stocks, because they have lost faith in their own ability to pick stocks. (Actually, there probably wasn't *anything* wrong with their stock selection. *It was their timing that was off.* They should have acted earlier. . .bought earlier in Stage One and either sold earlier before the emotional peak of Stage One or held on tightly right through the Stage One correction and *on up again* in the Stage Two Bull Market move.

If you are going to get involved in this Bull Market at all it is important to you, your money, your family, your security and your peace of mind that *you maintain your perspective at all times.* TRUE ! Unless you resist your own emotions. . .whether they be fear during much of the upswing or greed near the top of each move. . .your chances of making and keeping money in this Super Bull Market are going to be somewhere between slim and none. **THE FACT IS THAT REMARKABLY FEW INVESTORS MAKE MUCH MONEY EVEN DURING WILD BULL MARKETS.** Most People react to events late in the game. The secret of making money is to *anticipate* events, rather than react to them.

By and large, in our own newsletters we prefer to be a little *early* in all of our moves, whether buying or selling. What this often brings us is notes from subscribers telling us that they are (1) amazed at how right we have been until now and (2) sorry that we are so wrong "this time." We do *not* argue with our subscribers. It is their money. We tell them what is going on and what is coming next. Usually after they have gone against our view of the economy and the Market once or twice *they are more disposed to listen to us.* Then we start getting notes from them saying how pleased they are at their results, how happy they are to know and understand what is really going on for the first time, and often how amazed their friends and relatives are at their insights into coming Market moves. *The real test, of course, will come later on - when we tell them to get out of the Market during the frothy, emotional final run-up of Stage Three*. . .usually a time when Investors throw all caution to the winds and invest every penny they own or can borrow. If they listen to us then, we'll feel that we have *really* helped them !

CHAPTER ELEVEN
Do We Really Have To Live Through Another 1929 ?

NO ! That's the answer to the question above. No, we don't have to live through "Another 1929 !" It's possible that we will, of course. If not this time then some other time. . .*maybe 33 years from now*. But saying it is possible under certain sets of circumstances is a very long way from saying it must happen. The very same fears (of Another 1929) were expressed back in the 1950's. *People tend to forget today just how frightened Wall Street was in the early 1950's* as the Dow-Jones Industrial Average broke free from a long plateau under the 200 level and doubled in just four years. It got back to the previously unthinkable level (near 400) that had marked the 1929 top ! You would have thought the end of the World was at hand to listen to some of the fearful types on The Street!

But stocks rose right through 400 to 500. And again, there was in the Air talk of "Another 1929." But it didn't happen. Then "600" was reached. A correction. . .but still no collapse. "700" was next. Then "800." *Incredible!* The stock market had doubled and doubled again in the 1950's. The same 300% gain that had marked the end of the Bull Market, the end of the Super-Boom. . .almost the end of Western Civilization in 1929! Yet there were no real signs of speculative excess. Inflation was very low. Business was a long way from being over-expanded. Debt totals were under strict control (partly because Ike actually encouraged periodic recessions and stock market corrections).

John F. Kennedy replaced Eisenhower in the White House. To

the surprise of IKE himself (and many others), *JFK maintained the same strict control over debt and inflation that had marked the 1950's.* The Market dipped, then moved up to 900. Early in LBJ's Presidency it flicked at the 1000 level for the first time. And don't think 1000 didn't scare the bejeebers out of Wall Street. *1000! That's 10 times the 100 level that the Dow had touched on the downside just 24 years earlier (*right after Pearl Harbor). TEN TIMES! Surely *this* was "Another 1929"... that's what many People said. They were wrong. It's true that the Market couldn't really break much above that 1000 level until 1983 - *17 years later!* But neither did the Market's corrections fall back anything like the 90% that had made 1929-1933 such an unpleasant time-period to live through. During the 5 full years ending in 1983, for example, the Dow moved up and down like a yo-yo in a *fairly tight* band marked by 740 on the bottom and 1040 on the top. . .just 150 points above and below an implied 890 midpoint.

One of the reasons we did not have another "1929" at the end of the 1950's, at least in our humble opinion, is precisely because so many People had been so worried about "Another 1929" all during the 1950's. They never did lose their fear of debt and speculation! And so *they avoided the very kinds of excesses that had caused the crash in 1929.*

Now, we have to tell you that at least until this point in the 1980's, there is still enough genuine fear of "Another 1929" floating loose on Wall Street and indeed all over America (and Canada) so that - once again - the kinds of excesses that led to 1929 have largely been avoided.

As late as December, 1985, the Stock Market was selling at only 50% of its 1966 level after you adjust out inflation. There is one heck-of-a-lot of catching up to do here just to get back to that level first touched some 20 years ago. *Think about that!* TWENTY YEARS! The Stock market in 1966 was 10 times its level of TWENTY-FOUR YEARS EARLIER. Now a lot of People are worried out of their sleep because there is talk that the Dow may reach a point just double its mark of 20 years ago. DOUBLE! *And when you adjust for inflation the doubling is gone. 2000 on the Dow will mean that the Stock Market has regained just about one-half of the loss to inflation since 1966.* 3000 on the Dow would mean that the Market has made up for inflation and is back where it was in 1966. It still wouldn't account for any of the REAL growth and expansion in population, production and profit since 1966. To reflect that would require the Dow going even higher. . .say 4000 or more. Yet still the Market wouldn't be up in areas that *automatically* require and even demand a correction such as we had in 1929-1933.

HAVING SAID ALL THIS, WE SUGGEST THAT YOU KEEP YOUR PERSPECTIVE AS WE MOVE LATER INTO THE 1980's AND HIGHER IN THIS BULL MARKET. Remember, the *safest* gains probably come in the First Stage. That is behind us. The *biggest and longest-running* gains usually come in the Second Stage. (And as we write this to you we believe we are in that Middle Stage.) The *hottest-burning but most dangerous* gains tend to come in the Third Stage. And that is still ahead of us.

Our belief, and we will be stressing this belief in a couple of years, is that *you should cash some or all of your gains while the Third Stage is still burning white-hot. Hoard it safely. Wait patiently.* And use it to buy **BARGAINS** in real estate, stocks, businesses and the like during whatever correction *does* follow Stage Three !

Adrian Van Eck, America's
Number One Economic Forecaster
Since 1979, Says:

NOW HERE COMES 1927-28-1929 ALL OVER AGAIN!

A 3-Year Superboom -
(with the Dow crossing 3000)

Announcing:

If this book helps you realize that it is possible to see ahead in the economy with quite remarkable accuracy, you may well ask how you can build on this book's Foundation. *The answer can be found on Page 135.*

There you will find an offer of a Free Sample of Adrian Van Eck's remarkable monthly newsletter: *The Financial Research Center Forecast Letter,* yours with a no-risk trial.

The newsletter, like this book, is simple and easy to read. No special education or training is needed to share Adrian Van Eck's insights into coming trends. He says it is all the result of actions and re-actions by People and their money, both Public and Private. *For 7 consecutive years he has forecast the future with an accuracy that astounds his readers.*

Mail this form with your payment, today, to the FRC Forecast Letter, Financial Research Center, Inc., 5 Tripp Street, Framingham, Massachusetts 01701.

(New Readers Only!)   *Date* _____

   Yes! I want to take advantage of Adrian's trial offer. Enter my 2-month subscription. My check for $20(U.S.) is enclosed, payable to the FRC Forecast Letter.

Name (Print) _____

Address _____

City _____ State _____ Zip _____

BB-7

( ) One year at $150 U.S.

P.S. -- If you prefer a longer trial, check off the line
          above and make your payment for $150 U.S.

Here are Four Other FRC Letters For Investors

Table of Contents

See page 8
For Order Forms!

THE FINANCIAL RESEARCH CENTER
REAL ESTATE LETTER

ATTENTION: INVESTORS, BANKERS, BROKERS, MANAGERS, DEVELOPERS, CORPORATE PLANNERS, RENTERS, BUILDERS AND PROFESSIONAL ARCHITECTS.

You Are Cordially Invited To Become A Charter Discount-Rate Subscriber To Our New 8 Page Monthly letter For Those Who Buy, Sell, Finance, Design, Organize, Produce Or Use Real Estate!

The Editors Financial Research Center's *Tax-Law* Letter warned us months ago that "tax reform" was going to turn *Real Estate investing* upside-down in The United States of America.

Thus forewarned, we began to prepare for the day when *everyone connected with Real Estate* in any of the capacities above would be asking not only us but each other WHAT IS GOING ON HERE?.....*WHAT DOES IT MEAN FOR AMERICAN REAL ESTATE FOR ..1987...1988...AND 1989?* As we assembled a team of experts (more on this in a moment) it became obvious that changes are about to take place in American Real Estate of such a magnitude and of such *speed and duration* that not a single man or women connected with Real Estate in any way can hope to escape involvement. *Nothing like this complete turning-upside-down of Real Estate has ever happened before in America in such a short time span!*

We decided to publish a Newsletter on Real Estate for one very simple reason: when we started our serious research on the subject *we spent several hundreds of dollars to subscribe to all the letters we could find dealing with real estate.* NOT ONE OF THEM -- NO MATTER WHAT THE PRICE -- COULD ANSWER THE QUESTIONS WE HAD ABOUT REAL ESTATE FOR THIS YEAR, NEXT YEAR AND THE YEARS AFTER THAT.

We decided that if such a Letter did not exist, then we would research it...shape it...write it...edit it...publish it. *We are able..because of our size and the number of subscribers we knew we would attract at once after our announcement to keep our price down to a rock-bottom $82.50 a year. And now, during our introductory announcement period, we are offering an additional 40 % discount...all the way down to $49.50 (Only $85 (U.S.) for 2 years.)*

When you subscribe today, we will rush you as your complimentary bonus Free Of Extra Cost our Special Introductory Report on *THE* NEXT THREE YEARS IN AMERICAN REAL ESTATE.

You'll see why we talk seriously about the *biggest* single-year of building and selling single family homes in U.S. history......even bigger than the *SuperBoom years after World War Two*, when the GI's came home and wanted a place of their own in the suburbs. You'll see *why commercial real estate* (with tax shelters ended) *will revert back to the positive-cash-flow INCOME investments* they used to be in the "Old Days" - changing all the rules fast! You'll see which areas will be hot...(some *surprises* here!)

Because Real Estate has nearly as many facets as a diamond, *we have assembled a diverse Board of Editors to prepare our new Letter each month. We started with a veteran professional from New York City... an experienced and gifted executive who travels around The United States constantly to examine and evaluate commercial real estate properties.* He brings a complete knowledge of the current market for investment real estate, 'an up-to-the-minute awareness of the switch from tax shelters to income investments. *He Knows financing, marketing and management inside-out!*

We added the practical hands-on outlook of a rising *young developer of residential property in what is (surprisingly enough) one of the hottest home-building areas in The U.S. today....Southern Maine.* A graduate of (Ivy League) Dartmouth College and winner of a Master's Degree from world-famous Massachusetts Institute of Technology's Sloan School of Management, *he left a promising career in financial planning with an important New England hi-tech firm to pursue his heart's desire...building homes!*

Then to round out our team we enlisted the services of a *brilliant investment manager from The Middle West.* This uncommonly able 39-year-old financial professional holds a Master's from The University of Chicago. (*He was a disciple of Milton Friedman in Prof. Friedman's lesser-known and we think better days.*) This *member of our Board of Editors has been writing on real estate investment for years...but only to a small audience of wealthy private investors.* After reading through copies of his letters, and seeing how *accurate he has been in predicting major trends in real estate before they actually happened,* we knew he was just the man we were looking for to complete our Special Real Estate Team!

NOW WE ARE BLENDING THE BACKGROUNDS, TALENTS AND ENERGIES OF THESE THREE MEN WITH THOSE OF OUR OWN STAFF OF INVESTMENT PROFESSIONALS. THE RESULT IS A NEW 8 PAGE MONTHLY LETTER ON REAL ESTATE!

To kick off our new Letter, we have asked our Board of Editors to prepare a *Special BONUS REPORT on THE NEXT THREE YEARS IN AMERICAN REAL ESTATE.* We will send you a copy of this Bonus Report free of extra cost when you *subscribe today to our new Letter.*

See order form on page 8

THE FINANCIAL RESEARCH CENTER
INVESTMENT LETTER

ANNOUNCING:

A Special 40% Discount Offer By Our Affiliated Investment letter...If you Act Now!

(One year at $49.50 (U.S.) regular $82.50 value.
Two years at $85 (U.S.) regular $165 value!)

As you know, we began publishing a supplementary Investment Letter in September, 1985 at a point we felt would prove to be a major market bottom.(It was!) It was designed for those investor/subscribers who wanted *guidance in applying the Forecasts in our basic monthly Letter.*

Over the months, we have added features to The FRC Investment Letter. And we have added some *valuable, experienced Staff members* to assist in researching and writing it.

Our Investment letter was practically alone, when the Dow was at 1450 and falling, in predicting the the Dow would turn up explosively in late 1985...and reach 2000 by the end of 1986. (We were off by only five trading days!) Now we predict 3000 on the Dow in 18 to 24 months, and we are recommending a model portfolio of stocks we think can go up even faster...75% to 100% during this bull move!

AND THEN WE SUGGEST YOU TURN TO PAGE 8 AND TO TAKE FULL ADVANTAGE OF OUR *SPECIAL NEW DISCOUNT OFFER.*

4

THE FINANCIAL RESEARCH CENTER
TAX-LAW LETTER

IS THERE LIFE FOR TAX SAVINGS UNDER THE NEW TAX-REFORM LAW?

(Announcing a 16-page monthly Mini-Letter for only $24.75 a year)

There is no denying that the sweeping nature of *the new Tax Reform Bill has done away with a great many tax shelters we in America earlier took for granted.*

But there are still on the tax-law books hundreds and hundreds of *provisions that offer you and your family opportunities to minimize your Federal tax payment. It would be folly for you to ignore them* just because the *top rate* has been reduced. Also, *total Dollars involved* make it more than worth your while to stay on top of IRS Tax rulings and regulations - as well as Tax Court decisions. For *these often-overlooked additions to Tax Law tend to flesh out the Skeleton of TAX-LAW REFORM, answering the many questions that arise whenever such radical changes occur in our basic Tax Laws!*

OUR EDITORS CONTINUE, TO COVER ACTIONS IN CONGRESS, THE IRS, THE WHITE HOUSE AND THE FEDERAL TAX COURTS TO REFORM, REVISE, AMEND, CHANGE OR EVEN REPEAL ANY TAX LAW. And we track new ideas in Congress to Raise Tax Revenues.

And now, in addition to the above continuing features of The FRC Tax-Law Letter, we have *added* an experienced Tax Accountant to our Staff. Mr. James M. Lagerbom, C.P.A. a tax specialist who was formerly a partner in a CPA firm is now Financial Vice President here at The Financial Research Center, and is now writing six pages of vital, specific, factual tax reduction suggestions and recommendations each month...*six pages that may help you hold onto hundreds even thousands of extra dollars this year*. See **order form page 8.**

THE FINANCIAL RESEARCH CENTER
SPECIAL SITUATIONS LETTER

THE EDITOR OF THE FRC SPECIAL SITUATIONS LETTER, *HAVING DONE FAR BETTER THAN THE DOW-JONES INDUSTRIAL AVERAGE THIS YEAR,* HAS NOW OUTDONE HIMSELF, IN OUR OPINION. AFTER WEEKS OF SEARCHING, SIFTING AND EXAMINING U.S. HIGH-TECHNOLOGY STOCKS WITH STRONG EXPORT POTENTIAL, *HE HAS COME UP WITH A STOCK - IN HIS NEW MONTHLY REPORT - THAT BRINGS OUR OWN FORECASTS VIVIDLY TO LIFE. WE URGE YOU TO SEND FOR HIS SPECIAL SITUATIONS LETTER TODAY...AND GET HIS NEW REPORT FREE OF EXTRA COST AS YOUR COMPLIMENTARY GET-ACQUAINTED BONUS:*

In March, 1986 we proudly announced our new Special Situations Letter. And we installed as Executive Editor Walter C. Ramsley, a gifted and sensitive veteran of service as Editor at a very large and very important New York City investment advisory publishing firm. Then, *just about six months ago, we told you how pleased we were to report that he had finally gotten the Big Apple out of his system enough so that he could take seriously our own shall-we-say eccentric way of looking at the Economy.* We said that because he had chosen a kind-of-offbeat stock...one engaged in marketing land for housing development in out-of-the-way areas such as Northern New England. This fit one of our strongly-held beliefs about the direction the U.S. economy was headed.

6

Looking back, we see that Mr. Ramsley's selections have already grown by an average of 30% -not bad considering special situations usually require patience while they work out .(His very first stock selection, rose 150% in 10 months

Now our Special Situations Editor has pleased us mightily again. Knowing as he does our deep conviction that *high-technology* capital goods will hold the key to America curbing imports and greatly expanding exports, he has come up with a $5 stock that *sure does look to us* like it is on its way to being a real winner in exactly this field. He is featuring this little-known but well-run and importantly-backed SPECIAL SITUATION.

Our Special Situations Editor points out that this new selection is a very good *example of America's strengths, as contrasted with Japan's weaknesses.* Japan probably couldn't produce a company like this. Its system of lifetime employment at giant corporations, its heavy Govenment hand in research and development (stifling conceptual breakthroughs) and its relative lack of venture capital for start-ups all work against such companies. *In this case we have a proven entrepreneur-founder with good backing, excellent research and very bold marketing. Its sales have doubled in a year to $32.6 million. Down the road we see even faster growth in sales and earnings.* Its products are not only advanced, they are easy to learn and operate and increasingly cost effective. *We think this stock can triple, even quadruple! See order Form page 8.*

Pin your check(s) to this order from and mail today to:

The Financial Research Center, Inc.

Subscription Department, 5 Tripp St., Framingham MA 01701

☐ **THE FRC REAL ESTATE LETTER**

YES! Enter my subscription to your *new 8* page monthly Letter... THE FRC REAL ESTATE LETTER. My check is for the term I prefer: $75(U.S.) for one year, or $135(U.S.) for two years, I understand you will send me as my *introductory bonus free of extra cost* your new Special Report on THE NEXT THREE YEARS IN AMERICAN REAL ESTATE.

NAME (Please Print) _____

ADDRESS _____

CITY ___RE1-r3___ ZIP _____

☐ **THE FRC INVESTMENT LETTER**

YES! I want to take advantage of your subscription offer for your affiliated supplementary service, The FRC Investment Letter. *My check is enclosed for the term I prefer: One year (12 issues) at $75   Or two years (24 issues) at $135* . I understand that if I mail my check at once you will send me your current FRC Investment Letter FREE OF EXTRA COST AS A BONUS...and my subscription term will start with your next issue.

NAME (Please Print) _____

ADDRESS _____

CITY ___IL-r3___ Zip _____

☐ **THE FRC TAX-LAW-LETTER**

YES! *Enter my subscription today* to your Mini-TAX-LAW-LETTER for the term I prefer. My check is enclosed for $75 U.S. (one year) - or for $135 U.S. for two years.

NAME (Please Print) _____

ADDRESS _____

CITY ___TL-r3___ Zip _____

☐ **THE FRC SPECIAL SITUATIONS LETTER**

YES! Please enter my subscription today for your monthly FRC SPECIAL SITUATIONS LETTER. My check is enclosed for the term I prefer (U.S. funds): $225(U.S.) for one year, Or $405(U.S.) for two years. PLEASE RUSH ME AS MY COMPLIMENTARY GET-ACQUAINTED BONUS YOUR CURRENT LETTER FEATURING A $5 STOCK THAT YOU BELIEVE HOLDS GREAT PROMISE IN COMPUTER-AIDED ENGINEERING SYSTEMS.

NAME (Please Print) _____

ADDRESS _____

CITY ___SSL-r3___ Zip _____